SIMPLE HISTORY
A SIMPLE GUIDE TO

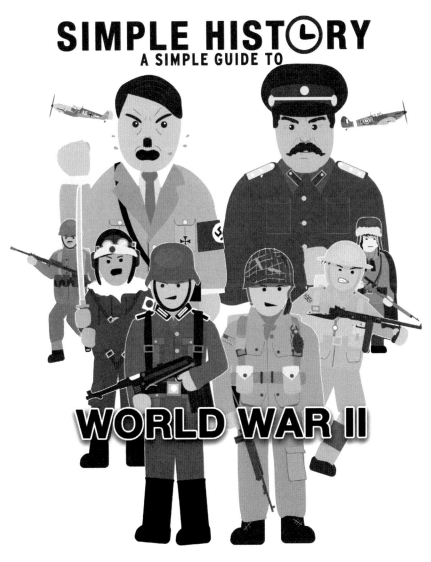

WORLD WAR II

Written and Illustrated by
Daniel Turner

CONTENTS

INTRODUCTION

On September 1, 1939 Nazi Germany fuelled by dictator Adolf Hitler, invaded Poland. The world was shocked.

The most destructive war in history had begun.

It would take six years for the Allies to become victorious and in that time millions would die for our freedom.

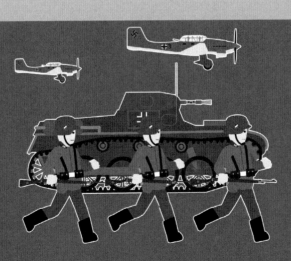

THE ROAD TO WAR

GERMANY IS PUNISHED 1919

Military. The German Army restricted to 100,000 men, 6 battleships and no air force. The Rhineland was also demilitarised.

Reparations. Germany had to pay 132 billion gold marks in war damages.

War guilt. Germany responsible for war damage.

Territory. Germany's colonies were taken away. Polish corridor created, dividing Germany in half.

Just after World War I, Germany's punishment was decided by the Allied forces. The crippled nation signed the 'Treaty of Versailles' with a number of clauses.

July 29, 1921

Hitler becomes leader of the NSDAP (Nazi) party. The party was becoming popular because of the problems in Germany caused by the Treaty of Versailles. Hitler also blames Jews and Communists for Germany's problems.

THE FÜHRER AND HIS ALLIES

January 30, 1933

In 1933 Hitler becomes Chancellor of Germany to President Hindenburg. Using his Brownshirt stormtroopers to intimidate voters Hitler is able to pass his Enabling Act law. Democracy is effectively ended in Germany and Hitler's Nazi dictatorship had begun.

From 1936 Germany joins forces with Italy and Japan forming the Axis powers.

ANSCHLUSS

March 12, 1938

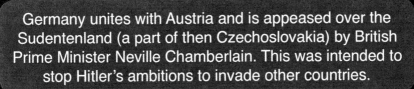

Germany unites with Austria and is appeased over the Sudentenland (a part of then Czechoslovakia) by British Prime Minister Neville Chamberlain. This was intended to stop Hitler's ambitions to invade other countries.

WORLD WAR 2

BLITZKRIEG INVASION!

September 1, 1939

On September 1, 1939 Germany invades Poland. Using the 'Blitzkrieg' tactic of fast, powerful attacks on the enemy Poland is soon in German hands. As Poland's allies, Britain and France declare war on Nazi Germany. What had made Hitler so confident? He had made the Nazi-Soviet Pact with Stalin in August promising not to go to war with Soviet Russia!

MINISTRY ● **OF FOOD**

RATION BOOK

1940–41

Surname _____

Other Names _____

Address _____

_____

Date of birth _____

IF FOUND RETURN TO

Rationing of food and resources starts in the UK on January 8, 1940. This was important because supply ships from America were being destroyed in high numbers by Germany.

WE SHALL NEVER

SURRENDER

Winston Churchill becomes the new British Prime Minister replacing Neville Chamberlain on the May 10, 1940. He inspires the country to fight on against the Nazis.

FRANCE
June 22,
1940

WESTERN EUROPE
IN
NAZI HANDS

HOLLAND

BELGIUM

In 1940 Hitler takes over Belgium, then Holland in a matter of days. Soon France also falls under Nazi control. The world is shocked at the speed of the invasion.

BRITAIN ON THE RETREAT

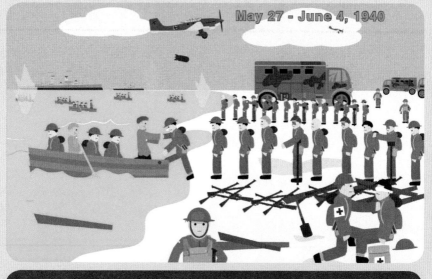

May 27 - June 4, 1940

Following the Allies defeat by the German Army in France, the British Expeditionary Force and the French Army is evacuated from Dunkirk.

July 10 - October 31, 1940

British victory in the Battle of Britain forces Hitler to postpone invasion plans.

THE BLITZ

September 7, 1940 -
May 21, 1941

LONDON NEWS

On September 7, 1940 Britain is bombed by German aircraft. Known as the 'Blitz', London and other cities become targets of these aerial raids. Factories were destroyed and civilians were killed during the terrifying attacks.

HITLER TURNS TO THE EAST

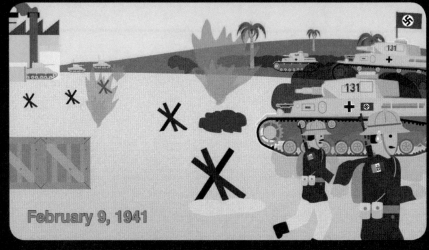

February 9, 1941

The British take Tobruk in North Africa, defeating the Italian forces there on February 9, 1941. Hitler sends a German tank force to fight back.

LENINGRAD

MOSCOW

UKRAINE

USSR

June 22, 1941

Hitler begins 'Operation Barbarossa' - the invasion of Soviet Russia. Stalin is surprised and underprepared.

DAY OF INFAMY
December 7, 1941

Aloha!

To stop Japan's empire expanding in the Pacific the USA stops supplying it oil. The Japanese react by attacking the U.S. fleet at Pearl Habour, bringing America into the war against the Axis.

THE FINAL SOLUTION
January 20, 1942

The elite guard of the Nazis, the SS, discuss the 'final solution' – a plan to mass murder the Jewish population. Jews are sent to concentration camps like Auschwitz, where they are imprisoned and killed in gas chambers.

Actung Min

PROBLEMS IN THE PACIFIC

Singapore speedily falls to the Japanese in February - around 80,000 British, Indian and Australians are taken prisoner.

The U.S. Navy win a decisive victory against the Japanese at the Battle of Midway, in June.

STALINGRAD

August 23, 1942 - February 2, 1943

The Battle of Stalingrad on the Eastern Front marks Germany's first major defeat. Fighting was ferocious as the city bore Stalin's name. Germany was always on the retreat afterwards.

Soviet soldiers used the sewer system to navigate and surprise the German Army.

German tanks often broke down and equipment was unsuitable for the Russian Winter. The Wehrmacht took enemy boots, coats and guns as they worked much better.

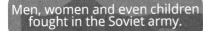

Men, women and even children fought in the Soviet army.

Sharpshooters on both sides took out enemy officers. They were celebrated for the high number of kills achieved.

Soviet troops are sent on suicidal charges against the enemy. Many were sent without a weapon and had to take one from the dead.

Stalin's NKVD officers executed anyone deserting the battle.

DESERT RATS DEFEAT THE FOX

In North Africa, British General Montgomery and his 'Desert Rats' defeat German General Rommel and his Afrika Korps. The North African campaign was over and now the Allies could move into Italy.

May 13, 1943

ITALY SURRENDERS

September 8, 1943

The Allies invade Sicily on July 10, 1943. The unpopular Mussolini is arrested and Italy surrenders in September.

From 1943 the Japanese are on the defence. British and Indian 'Chindits' use guerrilla tactics to push back the enemy.

D-DAY

On June 6, 1944 the Allies land on the beaches of Normandy, France. Americans assault Omaha and Utah beaches while Britain and Canada take Gold, Juno and Sword. A new western front is opened and the Allies liberate Paris in August. They now moved towards Germany.

Allied paratroopers drop behind enemy lines at night-time, early on June 6. They capture strategic objectives such as bridges and road crossings, to prevent a German counter attack.

"You are about to embark upon the Great Crusade, toward which we have striven these many months. The eyes of the world are upon you. The hopes and prayers of liberty-loving people everywhere march with you. "

Dwight D. Eisenhower

ISLAND HOPPING

The US Marines island hop towards the Japanese mainland. They take Guam on August 10, 1944 and then the volcanic island of Iwo Jima on March 26, 1945. On June 22, 1945 the Allies take Okinawa, an island very close to Japan. The Japanese forces ferociously use suicidal kamikaze attacks.

THE END OF THE REICH

The Soviets fight the last of the resisting German forces in Berlin from April 16 – May 2, 1945. During the battle Adolf Hitler takes poison with his wife Eva Braun and then shoots himself. Victory in Europe Day is celebrated on May 8, 1945.

April 30, 1945

Führerbunker - Vorbunker

ATOMIC BOMB

August 6, 1945

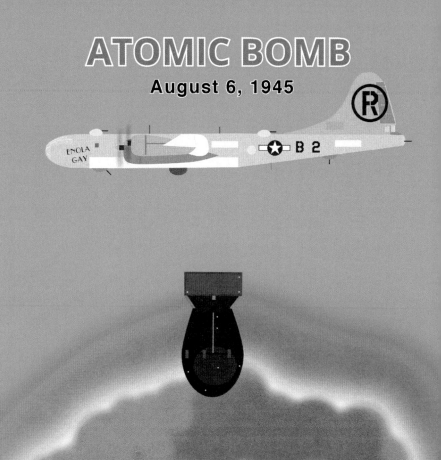

The Japanese Empire refuses to surrender to the Allies. America decides to use the newly developed atomic bomb for the first time. On August 6, 1945 the B-29 bomber 'Enola Gay' drops an atomic bomb on Hiroshima. The effects are devastating. Three days later a second atomic bomb is dropped on Nagasaki. On September 2, 1945 Japan surrenders and World War II is over.

FACTIONS & TECHNOLOGY

AXIS &

Benito Mussolini

Mussolini was the fascist leader of Italy who wanted a new Roman Empire. In 1935 he invaded Ethiopia and killed civilians with mustard gas.

He became friends with Hitler and formed an alliance with Nazi Germany. By 1941 the Italian Army was dependent on Germany for survival. Mussolini was unpopular with the Italians and was eventually shot and hung upside down in a petrol station!

Adolf Hitler

Hitler was the dictator of Nazi Germany. His Third Reich planned to expand Germany into a mighty empire and as commander-in-chief he commanded the German military during the war.

The war also saw his anti-Semitic ideas put into practice with the mass killing of Jews, called the Holocaust. Hitler became paranoid and reclusive when Nazi Germany started to lose the war. In April 1945, when the Soviets entered Berlin, he shot himself.

Hideki Tojo

Tojo was the militaristic Prime Minister of Japan from 1941. During the war he expanded the Japanese Empire into Asia and ordered the attack on Pearl Harbour.

When he realised that Japan could not win the war Tojo resigned in 1944. He shot himself in the chest, but survived. He was then executed for war crimes in 1948.

ALLIES

Winston Churchill

Churchill became Prime Minister of Britain in 1940. He made inspirational speeches to boost British morale when it looked like Nazi Germany would win.

As part of the 'Big Three' he worked with Franklin D. Roosevelt and Joseph Stalin to defeat Germany and Japan. He did not trust Stalin and refused to open a second front until 1944 (D-Day.)

Franklin D. Roosevelt

Roosevelt was the President of the United States of America. When Japan made a surprise attack on Pearl Harbour in 1941, Roosevelt delivered his famous 'Infamy Speech'.

The president died before the war had ended, leaving his successor Harry S. Truman to make the decision on dropping the first atomic bombs.

Joseph Stalin

Stalin was the harsh leader of Soviet Russia who killed millions of Russian peasants and purged many of his officials.

He made a Nazi-Soviet Pact with Hitler in 1939, splitting Poland between Russia and Germany. Hitler saw Communism as a great threat and turned on Stalin in 1941 by invading the USSR. He made sure that the Soviet Army was loyal to his dictatorship and had any deserters shot. After the war, Stalin took over Eastern Europe.

31

UNIFORMS & EQUIPMENT
THE PARATROOPER

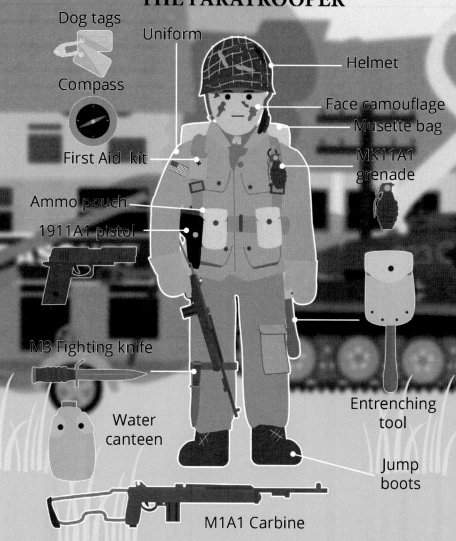

Dog tags

Uniform

Helmet

Compass

Face camouflage

Musette bag

First Aid kit

MK11A1 grenade

Ammo pouch

1911A1 pistol

M3 Fighting knife

Entrenching tool

Water canteen

Jump boots

M1A1 Carbine

On D-Day Allied paratroopers had to land behind enemy lines and slow down the German counterattack on the main invasion force. They were armed with weapons and equipment that would help them survive their dangerous mission.

32

British soldier
North Africa

British RAF pilot
Battle of Britain

Australian soldier
The Pacific

British paratrooper
D-Day

Canadian soldier
D-Day

Chindit
Burma

U.S. Soldier
D-Day

U.S Sailor
Pearl Harbour

U.S. paratrooper
D-Day

U.S. Marine
The Pacific

Soviet sniper
Stalingrad

French resistance
D-Day

German soldier
D-Day

Soviet soldier
Stalingrad

Italian Soldier
Sicily

**German
Afrika Korps**
North Africa

**German
MG42 gunner**
Stalingrad

**German
Waffen SS**
Berlin

**German
Tank commander**
D-Day

Japanese soldier
The Pacific

**Japanese
pilot**
Pearl Harbour

33

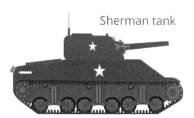

Sherman tank

Spitfire

TANKS

The development of tanks had come a long way since WWI. They were heavily armoured, had moving turrets and enormous firepower. The Allies made thousands of tanks like the Sherman, but they were weaker than the more powerful (but smaller in number) German tanks.

AIRCRAFT

Air superiority became extremely important in WWII. Fast and evasive fighter planes such as the Spitfire were used to protect troops on the ground and attack enemy fighters and bombers. Heavy bombers with large crews took out strategic targets to slow down enemy production or lower morale.

Type VII submarine

SUBMARINES

German U-boats hunting in "wolfpacks" devastated supply ships coming across the Atlantic to Britain. The Allies eventually managed to crack German Enigma codes turning the tide on the U-boats.

SMALL ARMS

Advancements in stamping, riveting, and welding transformed small arms. The use of semi-automatic rifles like the M1 Garand and assault rifles like the StG 44 were first seen in WWII.

RADAR

Radar was a vital tool for defence. It could detect enemy aircraft and ships from a long distance away by bouncing waves off of it.

SHIPS

The aircraft carrier dramatically changed naval combat. As floating platforms, aircraft could take off from the carriers and attack strategic targets.

HMS Ark Royal

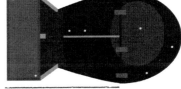

PENICILLIN

Penicillin was used widely during the war for treating infection. It is estimated to have saved 12-15% of Allied casualties.

88mm

ARTILLERY

Artillery caused a huge number of infantry casualties, destroyed aircraft and sunk ships. One artillery gun that was feared greatly by the Allies was the German 88, capable of taking out anything that was in range.

TOP SECRET

ATOMIC BOMB

Once Japan saw the effects of the atomic bomb on their nation they surrendered outright. The United States was the first to drop this destructive weapon, which could wipe out an entire city.

TOP SECRET

V-2 ROCKET

The first ballistic missile, V-2 rockets were used late in the war by Nazi Germany on Allied cities. After the war was over the weapon was used as a basis for space rockets during the Space Race.

TOP SECRET

Messerschmitt Me 262

JET ENGINE

The Axis and the Allies secretly developed the first fighter jets which saw limited action in the war. Jet fighters were superior to propeller aircraft but it was too late in the war for them to make a big impact.

WWII INFANTRY WEAPONS

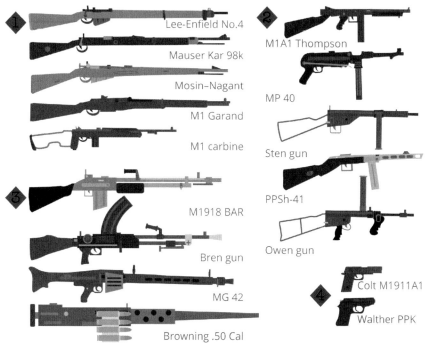

① Lee-Enfield No.4
Mauser Kar 98k
Mosin–Nagant
M1 Garand
M1 carbine

② M1A1 Thompson
MP 40
Sten gun
PPSh-41
Owen gun

③ M1918 BAR
Bren gun
MG 42
Browning .50 Cal

④ Colt M1911A1
Walther PPK

RIFLE
① Most infantry soldiers would have a rifle from the German Karabiner 98k to the British Lee Enfield. These guns were single shot, requiring the bolt to be opened and closed before firing. Later on gas operated semi-automatic rifles were used on the frontlines, like the M1 Garand. This was a great advancement, although the 8 round magazine had to be fired in its entirety and made a loud ping when ejected!

SUBMACHINE GUN
② A submachine gun is a fully automatic short range weapon that fires pistol ammunition. A popular submachinegun for the Allies was the Thompson. The German Army used the MP40 and Britain mass-produced the Sten gun which was cheaper but often jammed.

HEAVY & LIGHT MACHINE GUNS
③ Machine guns were used to defend fortified positions or to support an attack on the enemy objective. Heavy machine guns like the 50. Cal and the MG42 were mounted on tanks, aircraft and jeeps so the vehicle could be defended.

HANDGUN
④ Pistols were used by officers, tank crews and pilots. They were accurate only at close range.

WWII INFANTRY WEAPONS

StG44

M9A1 Bazooka

S-Mine 35

Mk 2 grenade

M2 flamethrower

Model 24 Stielhandgranate

M2 mortar

ASSAULT RIFLE
Invented by late war Nazi Germany, the Sturmgewehr 44 is the first assault rifle of its kind. It was accurate at long range like a standard rifle and at short range like a submachine gun. The StG 44 went onto inspire the AK47.

ANTI-TANK WEAPON
The US Army carried bazookas which could fire a 3.4lb rocket which if fired at the right spot could disable a tank.

FLAMETHROWER
The flamethrower is a weapon which shoots fire out of the nozzle and is fuelled by the gas canisters in the soldier's backpack. The weapon was used by the Allies and the Axis to clear out enemy bunkers and trenches. They also experimented with attaching flamethrowers to tanks and other vehicles.

GRENADE
Grenades are small bombs which explode after a few seconds of the pin being removed. WWII also saw the use of rifle grenades and homemade bombs called Molotov cocktails.

MINES
Mines were a kind of trap which exploded, wounding or killing the unlucky soldier who touched it.

PORTABLE MORTAR
Mortars were used to take out infantry. The projectile bombs are dropped down the tube and fired upwards where they land on the enemy, if targeted right.

PROPAGANDA

Propaganda posters encouraged people to do different things for the war effort and keep morale up.

On the left is 'Rosie the Riveter' an American poster which persuaded women to take up jobs in the munitions factories. In the middle is a 'Dig for Victory' poster which encouraged the British public to grow their own food to combat shortages. Lastly on the right is a Soviet poster called the 'Motherland is calling!'. It was created in 1941 to get people to fight and defend Russia from the invading German Army.

Joseph Goebbels was in charge of the Nazi propaganda machine. Through movies, radio, art, music, posters and rallies he made Hitler look great and Gemany's enemies look bad.

Everything had to be approved or censored to suit the Nazi party's message.

Goebbels poisoned himself shortly after Hitler's suicide on April 30, 1945.

THE WAR
EXPERIENCE

TROPICAL LIFE

Rain pouring down would make terrain marshy and slippery.

U.S. Marines could go for days without seeing the enemy but were constantly paranoid. A Japanese soldier could be hiding in the trees waiting to ambush or he may have laid booby traps.

'The 1000 yard stare' was a term describing the blank look that battle-weary soldiers gave.

Fighting in the Pacific theatre offered unique dangers for soldiers. The tropical environment looked nice from a distance but once you were on the island it was a different story..

Humidity and tropical diseases like malaria plagued Marines every day. Temperatures were above 100 degrees and water shortages meant thirst was a constant struggle.

The Japanese would often bomb supply ships. Marines might only have 2 meals a day or none at all.

FLYING FORTRESS

Strategic bombing was used to destroy weapon factories, shipyards and cities. The Royal Air Force bombed German targets during the night but the Americans went on bombing missions in broad daylight. This was more deadly but also more accurate in hitting enemy targets.

The B-17 'Flying Fortress' was used for long distance bombing missions. It could carry a lot of bombs and was armed to the teeth!

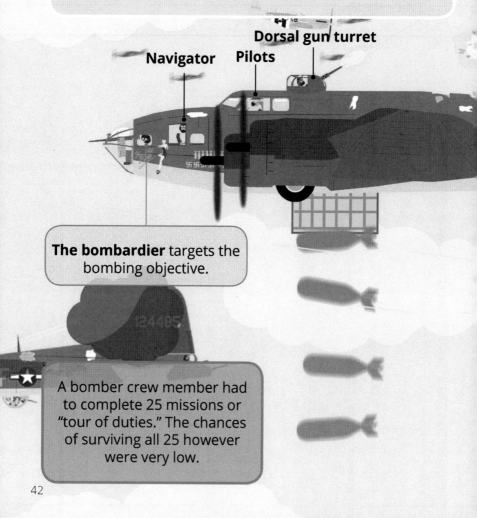

Dorsal gun turret

Navigator   **Pilots**

The bombardier targets the bombing objective.

A bomber crew member had to complete 25 missions or "tour of duties." The chances of surviving all 25 however were very low.

The tail gunner or 'tail-end Charlie' defended the bomber's rear. It was the most important turret and extremely vulnerable.

Waist gunners suffered the most casualties.

124485

The ball turret gunner was an uncomfortable, cramped position.

P-51 Mustang fighters escort the bombers, protecting them from the German Luftwaffe.

THE BRITISH HOME FRONT

Hitler bombed British cities (the Blitz) in order to lower civilian morale. He also destroyed supply ships bringing food in an attempt to starve the country into surrender. But the British homefront had a number of ways to survive this situation.

Civilians had to blackout their lights and windows so that the enemy aircraft couldn't spot their targets. Because of the lack of street lighting many people died in car accidents.

Food was grown in the garden as part of the 'Dig for Victory' campaign.

People built Anderson shelters in their back gardens. It was made from steel and would protect the family from shrapnel and debris.

WEEKLY FOOD RATIONS

As German U-boats tried to destroy food supply ships coming into Britain the government started rationing to make sure everyone got an equal share.

Bacon & Ham 4 oz	Milk 3 pints
Meat 1 s. 2d.	Sugar 8 oz
Butter 2 oz	Preserves 1 lb every 2 months
Cheese 2 oz	Tea 2 oz
Margarine 4 oz	1 Egg
Cooking fat 4 oz	Sweets/Candy 12 oz every 4 weeks

Wardens were brave volunteers who would get people into shelters, put out fires and help the injured.

An air raid siren would screech when German bombers were approaching.

THE HOLOCAUST

Hitler's plan was to remove Jews, Slavs, Gypsies and others from the world by placing them into death camps and murdering them. This was called the Holocaust.

When Nazi Germany invaded Soviet Russia death squads shot and killed innocent Jews. The leader of the SS, Heinrich Himmler however felt that the process was too slow. Their evil solution? Send them to execution camps to be killed in gas chambers.

The most infamous death camps were Auschwitz-Birkenau, Belzec, Sobibor and Treblinka. Victims would have their hair shaved for bed mattresses and any gold teeth removed. The prisoners were told that they were going to the showers but they were really going to the gas chamber where they would be exposed to the deadly chemical Zyklon B. Trees covered up the chambers to the other prisoners living in the bunkers.

ANNE FRANK'S DIARY

"I don't think of all the misery but of the beauty that still remains." **Anne Frank**

German-Jewish girl Anne Frank was only 13 years old when her family escaped to the Netherlands away from the Nazis. When the Nazis invaded Holland and started rounding up Jews, Anne and her family hid in an attic.

For 2 years she kept a diary, writing about the terrible things happening around her. In 1944 her family were discovered by the Nazis and were sent to a concentration camp. All of them except her father Otto, died. Anne's diary lives on as a unique account of the Holocaust.

As the Allies marched into Europe in 1945 they liberated many of the concentration camps. Nothing could prepare them for the shocking situation that had been left behind. Corpses lay out in the open. Survivors that were left were suffering from starvation and disease.

Overall this evil act in history killed over 6 million people.

WORLD WAR II
STATISTICS

September 1, 1939 – September 2, 1945

WWII DEATH TOLL 55 +MILLION

ALLIED MILITARY CASUALTIES
18,500,000
AXIS MILITARY CASUALTIES
6,000,000
TOTAL CIVILIAN CASUALTIES
30,500,000

FIRSTS:
- RADAR
- JET ENGINES

MASS USE OF
- PENICILLIN
- COMPUTER
- ATOMIC BOMB

DURATION
6 years and
1 day

VICTORY IN EUROPE DAY
MAY 8, 1945
VICTORY OVER JAPAN DAY
SEPTEMBER 2, 1945

*Approximate figures

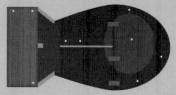

So how well do you know your Second World War history? Have a go below!

1) What event triggered the start of World War II?
(A) Germany invaded Poland (B) Japan attacks Pearl Harbour
(C) Hitler becomes Führer

2) What was the name of the German bombing of Britain?
(A) Kamikaze (B)The Holocaust (C) The Blitz

3) What was the Anschluss?
(A) Uniting Germany with Austria (B) A German military tactic
(C) The name of a German concentration camp

4) Who was the Japanese Prime Minister who ordered the Pearl Harbour attack?
(A) Koki Hirota (B) Keisuke Okada (C) Hideki Tojo

5) What was the name of the Allied invasion of Normandy on June 6, 1944?
(A) D-Day (B) Market Garden (C) Barbarossa

6) What year did Hitler invade Soviet Russia?
(A) 1939 (B) 1941 (C) 1942

7) What was the V-2?
(A) A jet fighter (B) A tank (C) A ballistic missile

8) What date was Victory in Europe day?
(A) May 8, 1945 (B) April 30, 1945 (C) September 2, 1945

How many answers did you get right?

∨ 1-3 PRIVATE- Oi! get back to boot camp!

⧫ 4-6 SERGEANT - time to lead the men, Sergeant

⧫ 7-8 LIEUTENANT - you are quite the military genius!

Answers: 1) A, 2) C, 3) A, 4) C, 5) A, 6) B, 7) C, 8) A

GLOSSARY

Allies
Countries including Britain, France, the USA and the USSR) who fought against the Axis.

Anschluss
Uniting Germany with Austria.

Appeasement
Giving Hitler a bit of what he wanted to avoid war.

Atomic bomb
A destructive weapon that could destroy a city.

Axis powers
Germany, Japan, Italy and other countries that fought against the Allies.

Blitz
The German bombing of Britain.

Blitzkrieg
German military tactic meaning 'lightning war'.

Chancellor
Head of the government.

Communism
Political system believing in the working class and equality.

Concentration camp
A prison where Jews and political prisoners were held.

D-Day
Allied invasion of Normandy, France.

Demilitarised
No military allowed in the area.

Dictator
A ruler with total power over a country.

Fascism
A government ruled by a dictator.

Final Solution
Nazi plan to kill the Jewish population.

Führer
Hitler's title as dictator.

Holocaust
Genocide of Jews by Nazi Germany.

Kamikaze
A Japanese suicidal attack.

Luftwaffe
The German air force.

Militaristic
Using military aggression.

Morale
How confident people feel they could win the war.

Nazi
The political part led by Hitler, short for 'Nationalist Socialist German Workers' Party'.

Pact
An agreement between two countries.

Propaganda
Using media to spread a political message.

Rationing
Ensuring there is enough food for everyone.

Reparations
When a country pays for war damage caused.

Soviet Union
Russia and other states following Communism.

SS
Elite Nazis which handled security and had its own army.

U-Boat
Name for a German submarine.

V-E Day
Victory in Europe Day. May 8, 1945.

V-J Day
Victory in Japan Day. September 2, 1945.

Wehrmacht
German armed forces.

INDEX

IN PRINT, TABLET AND E-BOOK FORMATS

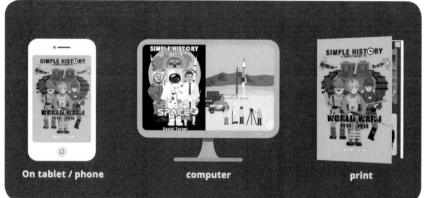

On tablet / phone   computer   print

SIMPLE HISTORY
GUIDES IN THE SERIES:

Simple History a guide to World War I
Simple History a guide to the Space Race
Simple History a guide to the Wild West
Simple History a guide to Henry VIII
Simple History a guide to Ancient Egypt
Simple History a guide to World War II
Simple History a guide to Elizabeth I
Simple History a guide to the Victorians
Simple History a guide to the American Revolution
Simple History a guide to Pirates
Simple Art Van Gogh
Simple Geography Brazil

www.simplehistory.co.uk

AVAILABLE NOW AND COMING SOON!

Made in the USA
Middletown, DE
09 July 2019